LIVING IN... ITALY

by Chloe Perkins
illustrated by Tom Woolley

READY-TO-READ

SIMON SPOTLIGHT

An imprint of Simon & Schuster Children's Publishing Division • New York   London   Toronto   Sydney   New Delhi • 1230 Avenue of the Americas, New York, New York 10020 • This Simon Spotlight edition February 2016 • Text copyright © 2016 by Simon & Schuster, Inc. Illustrations copyright © 2016 by Tom Woolley • Additional artwork by Reg Silva

Library of Congress Cataloging-in-Publication Data
Perkins, Chloe. • Italy / by Chloe Perkins ; illustrated by Tom Woolley; additional artwork by Reg Silva. pages cm. — (Living in .. series) At head of title: Living in ... • "Read-to-read." • 1. Italy—Juvenile literature. I. Woolley, Tom, 1981- illustrator. II. Silva, Reg, illustrator. III. Title. IV. Title: Living in ...
DG417.P46 2016 945—dc23 • 2015014960
ISBN 978-1-4814-5201-4 (hc) • ISBN 978-1-4814-5200-7 (pbk) • ISBN 978-1-4814-5202-1 (eBook)

GLOSSARY

Barbarian: a group of people from Northern Europe, outside the Roman empire, who defeated the Romans in 476 CE

City-state: a type of government in which a central city rules itself and the land around it

Era: a long span of time that is named for something important that happened during that time, such as the era of the Roman empire

Festival: a celebration of a special person, event, holiday, or belief

Musical notation: a set of instructions written for playing music

Opera: a play that is told mostly or entirely through song

Overthrow: to take control of a country by force

Region: a place with certain geographic features that make it different from the surrounding area

Tradition: something, such as a belief or practice, that has been passed down within a group for a long time

Unite: to join together as one

NOTE TO READERS: Some of these words may have more than one definition. The definitions above are how these words are used in this book.

Ciao! (say: chow)
That means "hi" in Italian.
My name is Pia,
and I live in Italy.
Italy is a country in Europe
where about sixty
million people live . . .
including me!

Italy is famous for
its shape.
Doesn't it look like
a boot?
The boot is kicking
Italy's two islands,
Sicily and Sardinia.

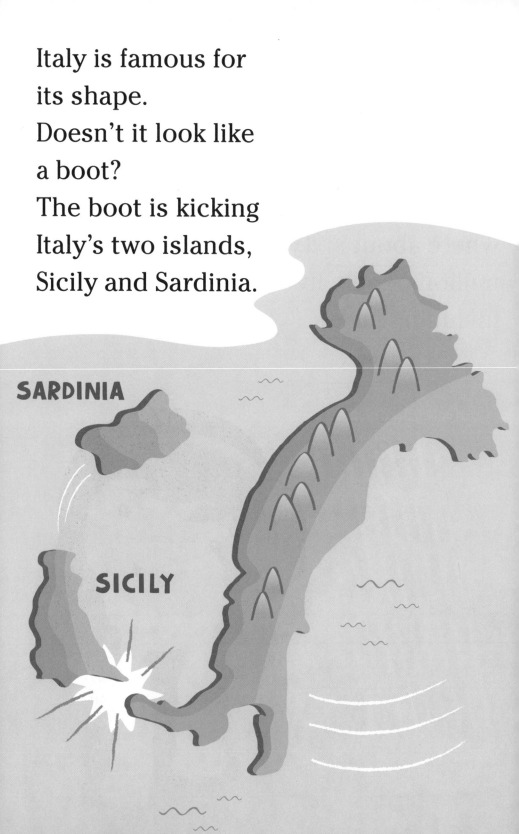

SARDINIA

SICILY

Sicily is home to five million
people! It's the biggest island
in the Mediterranean Sea.
Sardinia is smaller.
It has pretty beaches
and mountains.
I love going on vacation
there with my family.

Italy is split into twenty regions.
Each region has its own
government and traditions.
For example, in Tuscany
people eat very simple food.
But nearby in Emilia-Romagna,
people eat food with lots
of spices and flavors.

People in different regions
might celebrate different festivals
or wear different clothes or
listen to different kinds of music.
And while some regions are small,
many regions have big cities.

Venice is a city that was built on the water. People travel in boats instead of cars!

Pizza was first made in the city of Naples. This pizza is called Neapolitan pizza and can only be made using special ingredients.

Milan is Italy's fashion capital.
Four times a year Milan has a
fashion week for designers
to show off new clothes!
Florence is the city of art.
Many beautiful buildings,
sculptures, and paintings
can be found there.

I live in a city called
Foligno (say: Foh-LEEN-yo)
in the Umbria region.
Foligno is about one hundred
miles north of Rome,
the capital of Italy.

FOLIGNO

ROME

I live with my mom, dad,
grandma, and big brother
in a yellow house.
We have a black dog
named Luna.

My mom is a professor at
a university, and my dad
works for a museum.
My brother is in high school.
He loves playing soccer!
My grandma lives with us too.
In Italy many grandparents
live with their families.

And that's a good thing too,
because each morning
my grandma makes
us a delicious breakfast!
In Italy some people eat
sweet things for breakfast like
cookies, bread, and cakes.

After breakfast my dad
drives me to school.
There are fifteen kids
in my class.
My teacher checks attendance
and then we start our first
subject: history!
Italy has a long history.

So far I've learned about
the ancient people who lived
here before Italy was even
a country! People like the
Etruscans (say: Eh-TRUS-kans),
who built cities around 700 BCE.
The Etruscans were great sailors,
craftspeople, and warriors.

But history gets really interesting in 509 BCE. That's when people in the city of Rome overthrew their king and later defeated the Etruscans!

Rome built up its army
and defeated many nations.
At its height, the Roman Empire
was so big, it stretched
from England to Africa!
Rome was defeated by
barbarians in 476 CE.

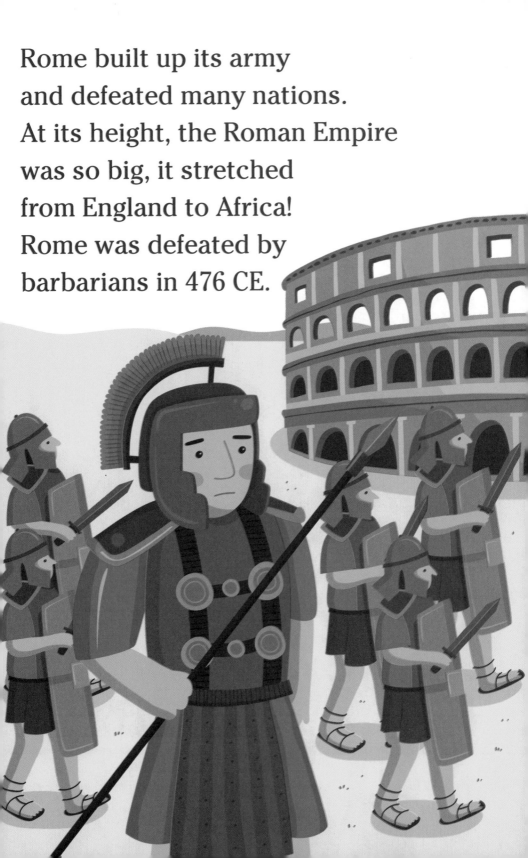

After Rome fell, the land
was split into city-states,
which were like tiny countries.
Bigger countries fought over
these city-states in the hundreds
of years that followed.

In the late 1700s, France defeated many city-states and brought them together. The French passed along new ideas about being loyal to your country.

When the French left
in 1814, their ideas stayed.
The Italians wanted to unite
their country. And in 1861,
the country of Italy was born!
By 1871, all the regions
we know today had
become part of Italy.

That's what we have
learned so far!
After the lesson, I put away my
history book and walk
to music class.

Music is very important in Italy.
Italy is the birthplace of opera,
the violin, and the piano.

Even musical notation,
the way we write music,
came from Italy!

Olivia and Sofia are
my best friends at school.
We all play violin in music class.
When I grow up, I want to be
the best violin player in Italy.

After music comes
science class.
Today we are learning
about how plants grow.

Many famous scientists and
inventors came from Italy.
Italians are credited with
inventing the radio, batteries,
and even eyeglasses!

On Mondays, Wednesdays, and Fridays,
school lasts until four thirty.
I take classes like math, reading,
art, English, and computers.

On Tuesdays and Thursdays,
school ends at lunchtime.
Since today is Tuesday,
I get to go home now!

At home my grandma
cooks lunch.
Sometimes we'll
eat a sandwich or
cooked fish with vegetables.
Today we're eating a crunchy
salad with chicken!

On Tuesdays and Thursdays
I take violin lessons
with our neighbor.
I practice every day
so I can get better.

When my brother gets
home from soccer
practice at his sports club,
he helps me with my
homework.
When we're done,
we play a quick
game of soccer.

It's time for dinner!
In Italy it's very important
to eat one meal each day
with your family.
Often we eat pasta and meat
that's cooked in a creamy sauce.
As we eat, we take turns
talking about our day.

After dinner I get ready for bed.
On my bedroom wall I have
a big map. I put a pushpin
on each country I want to visit.
Would you like to visit
Italy someday?
There are so many places
in the world to see!

ALL ABOUT
ITALY!

NAME: Italian Republic (Or Italy for short!)

POPULATION: 61 million

CAPITAL: Rome

LANGUAGE: Italian (German, French, and Slovene are commonly spoken in several regions)

TOTAL AREA: 116,348 square miles

GOVERNMENT: democracy, republic

CURRENCY: euro

FUN FACT: Italy has the most UNESCO World Heritage Sites of any other country in the world. Each site is protected and preserved so that future generations can visit it and learn more about world history. Italy's World Heritage Sites include the Dolomite Mountains, the city of Venice, and two ancient Etruscan cemeteries in the Lazio region.

FLAG: Three equal-sized vertical stripes of green, white, and red, commonly called the *Tricolore*. *Tricolore* means "tricolor" or "containing three colors" in Italian.